AF812270

My First Sinhala
Body Parts

Picture Book with English Translations

Published By: My First Picture Book™

A Heartfelt Message from Our Publishers:

Your support does more than just buy a book. It uplifts native authors and fuels the dreams of a close-knit business. We value every reader, and your insights could shape our next bestseller! Got suggestions or feedback? Let's co-create magic. Connect with us through the 'Contact Us' section on our website at **MyFirstPictureBook.com**.

Ankle

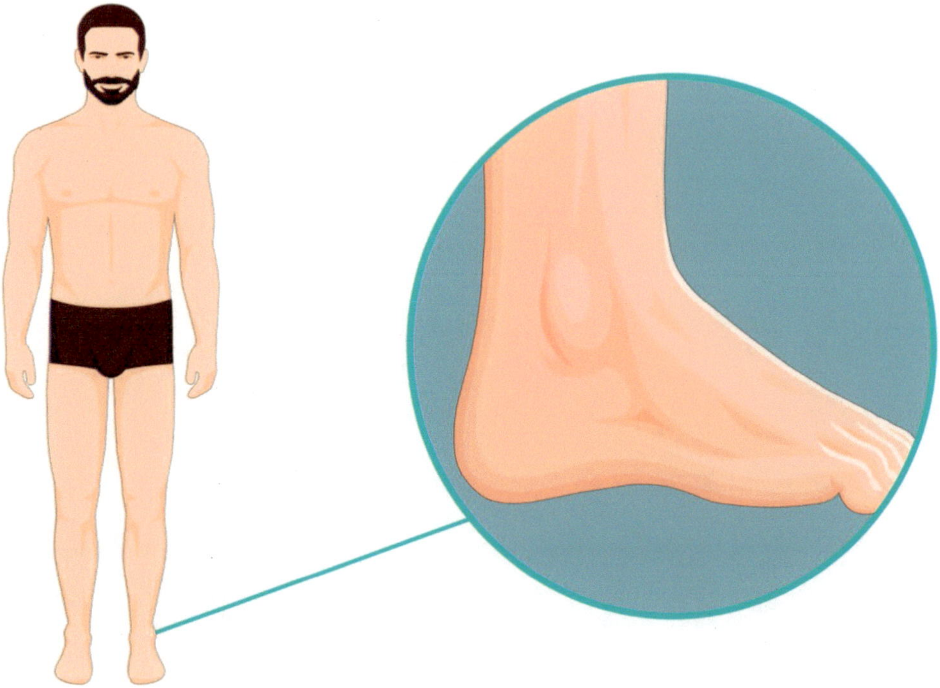

වළලුකර

va-la-lu-ka-ra

Arm

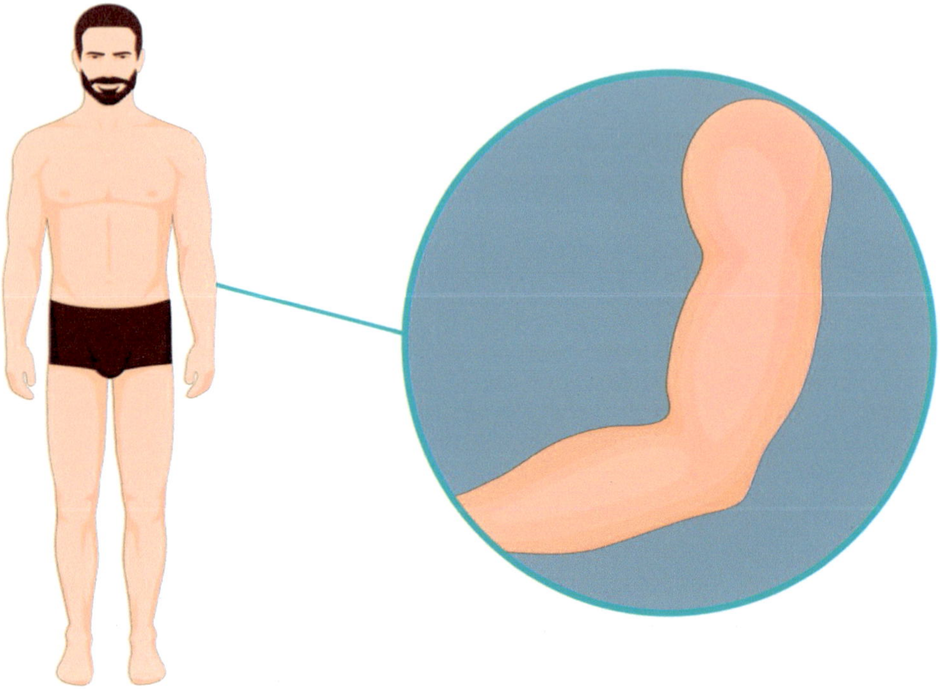

බාහුව

baa-hu-wa

Back

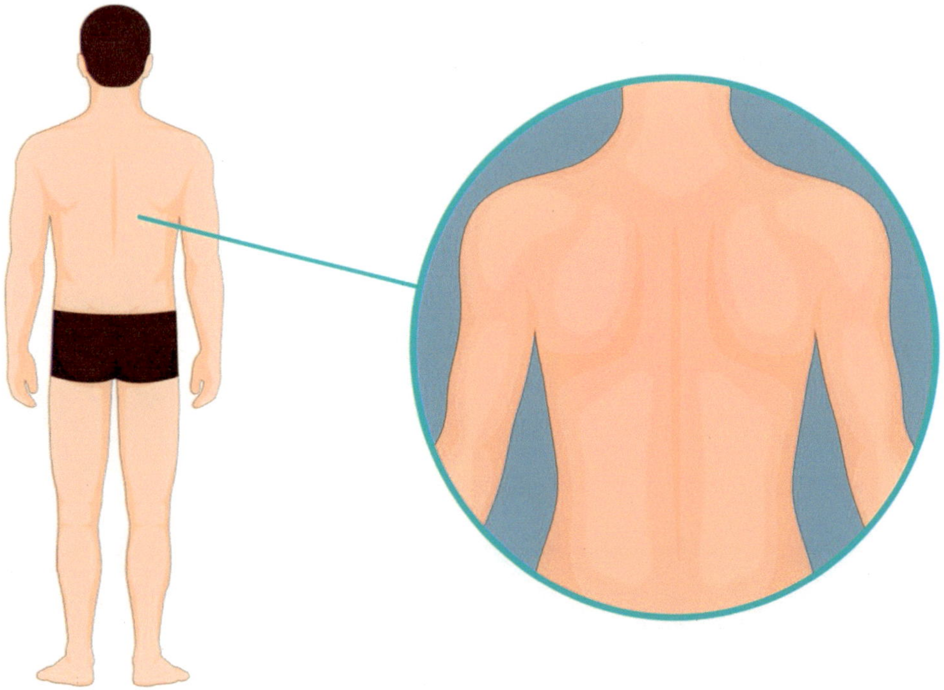

පිට

pi-ta

Beard

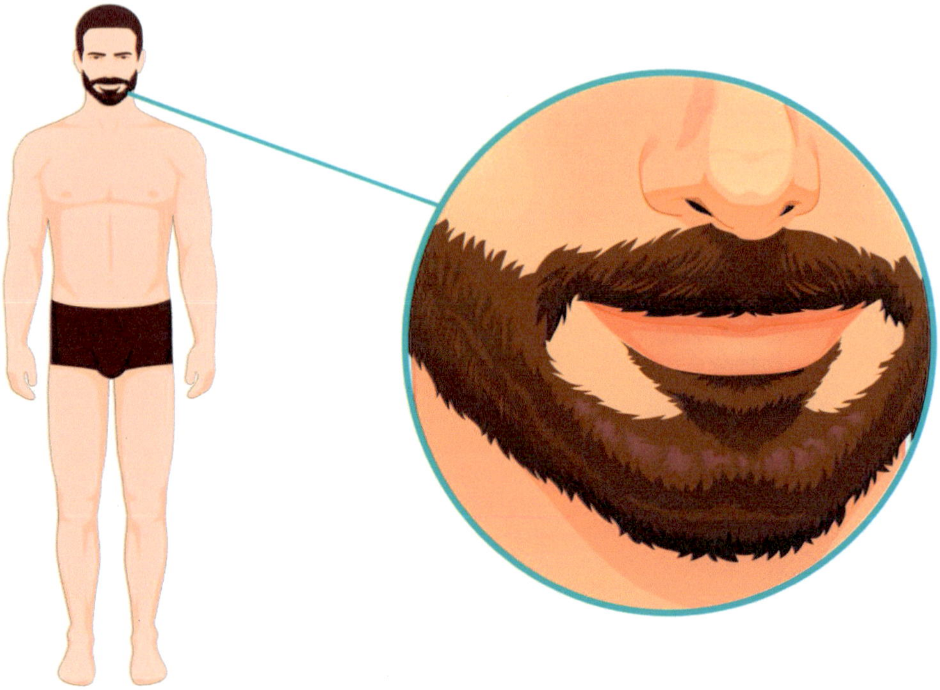

රැවුල

ra-vu-la

Brain

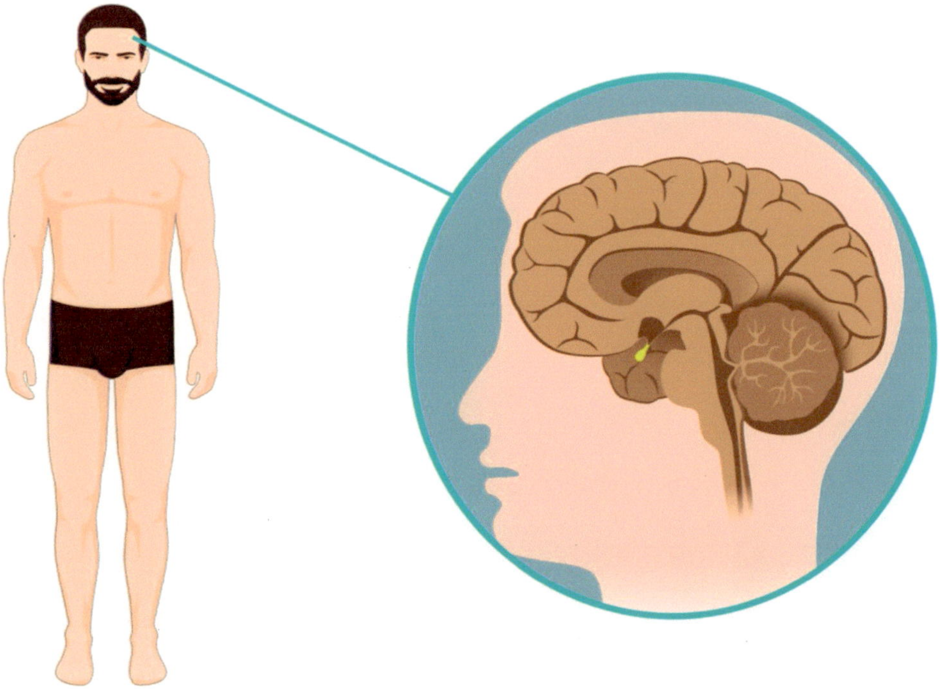

මොළය

mo-la-ya

Chin

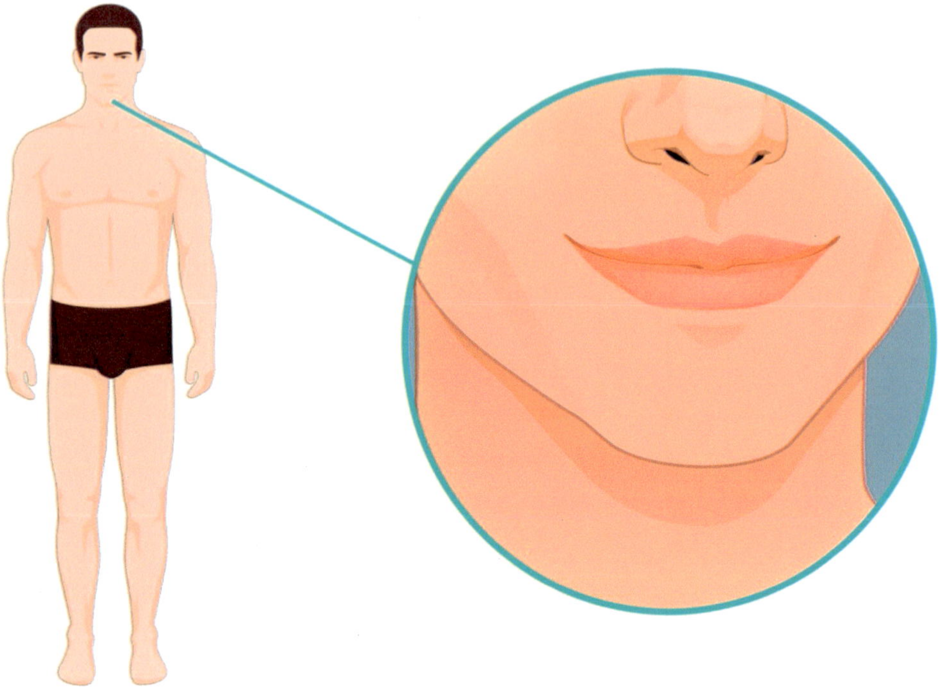

නිකට

ni-ka-ta

Ear

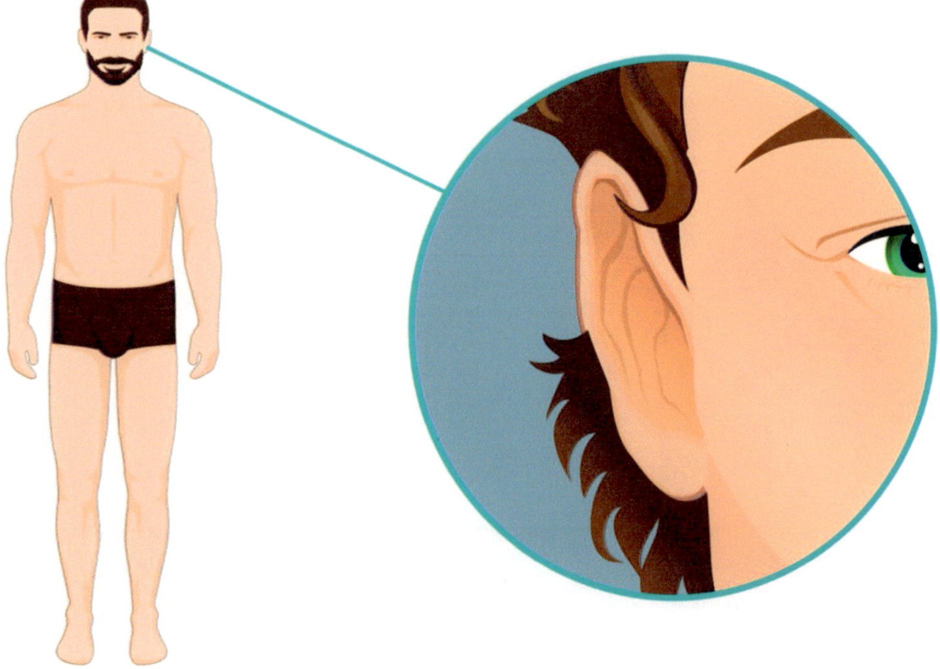

කන

ka-na

Elbow

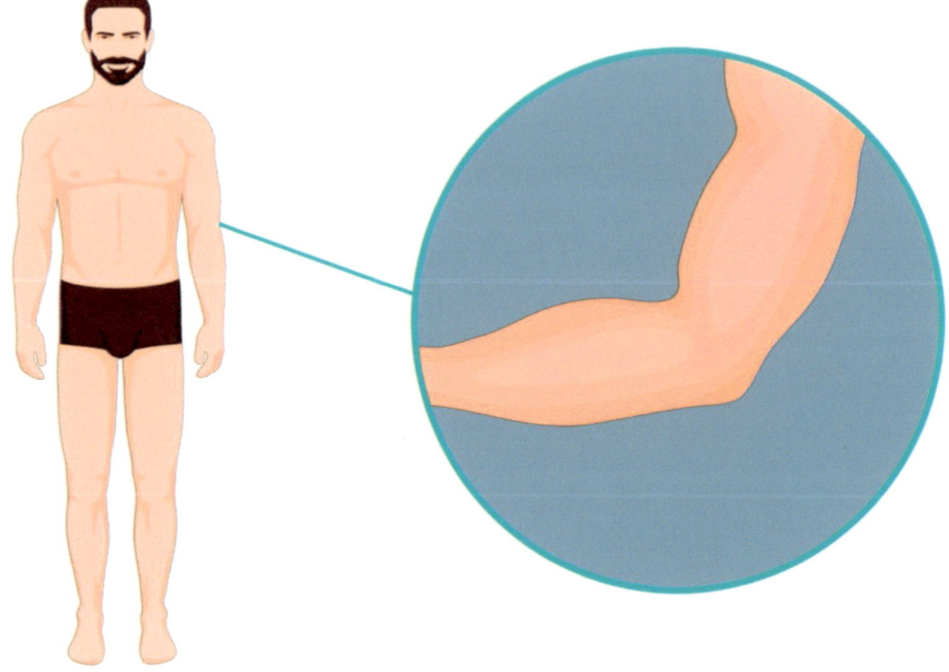

වැලමිට

vae-la-mi-ta

Eye

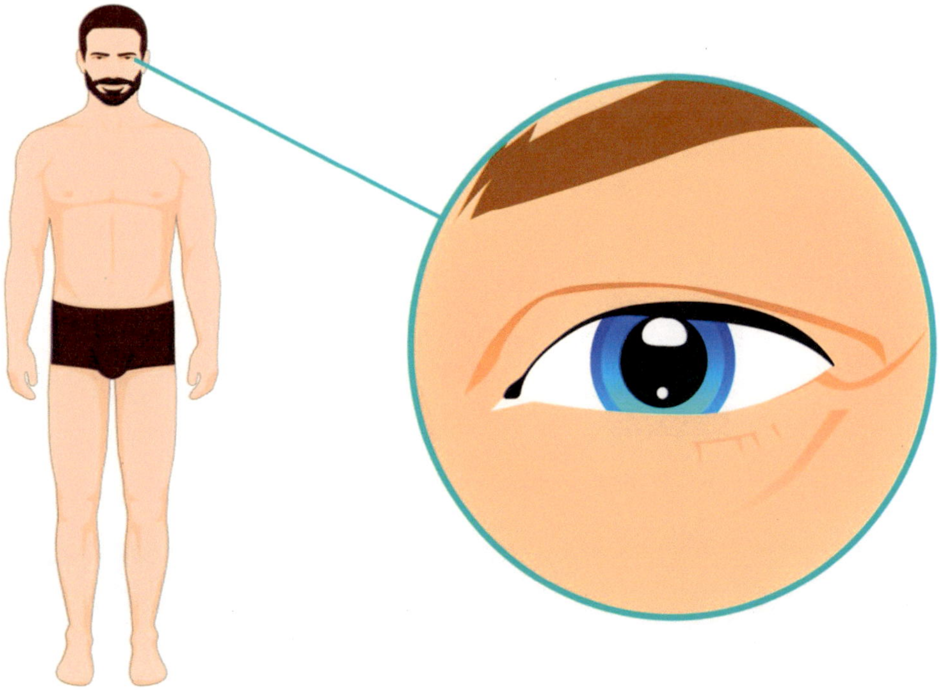

ඇස

ae-sa

Eyebrow

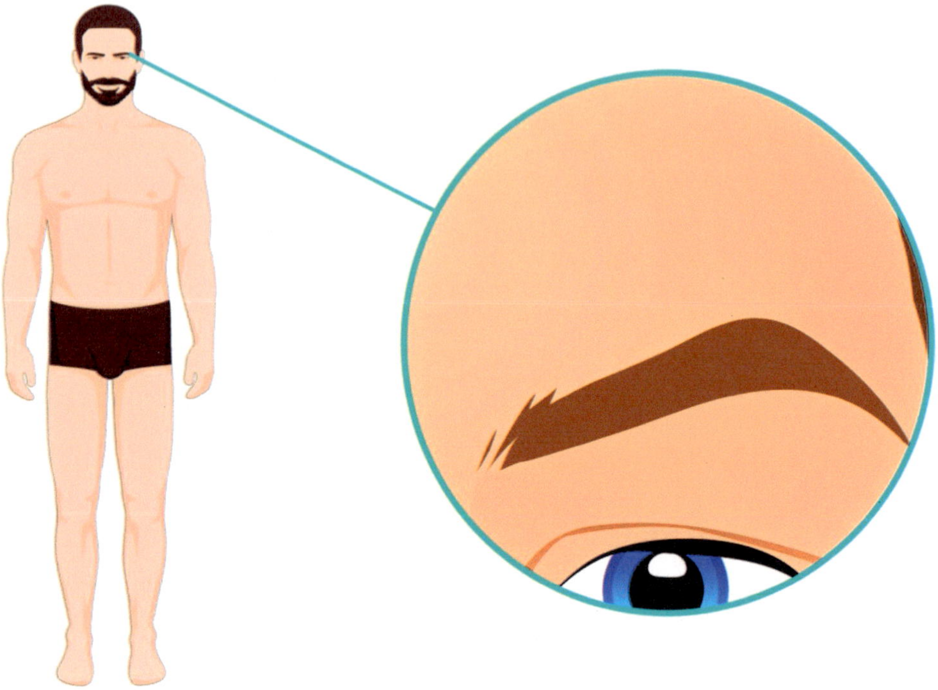

ඇහි බැම

ae-hi bae-ma

Face

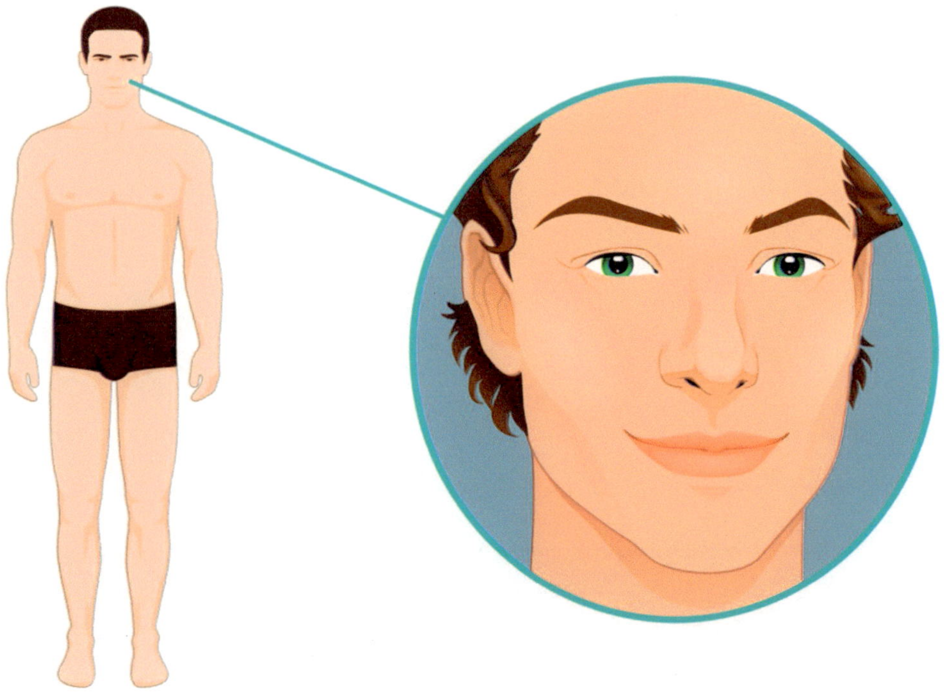

මුහුණ

mu-hu-na

Finger

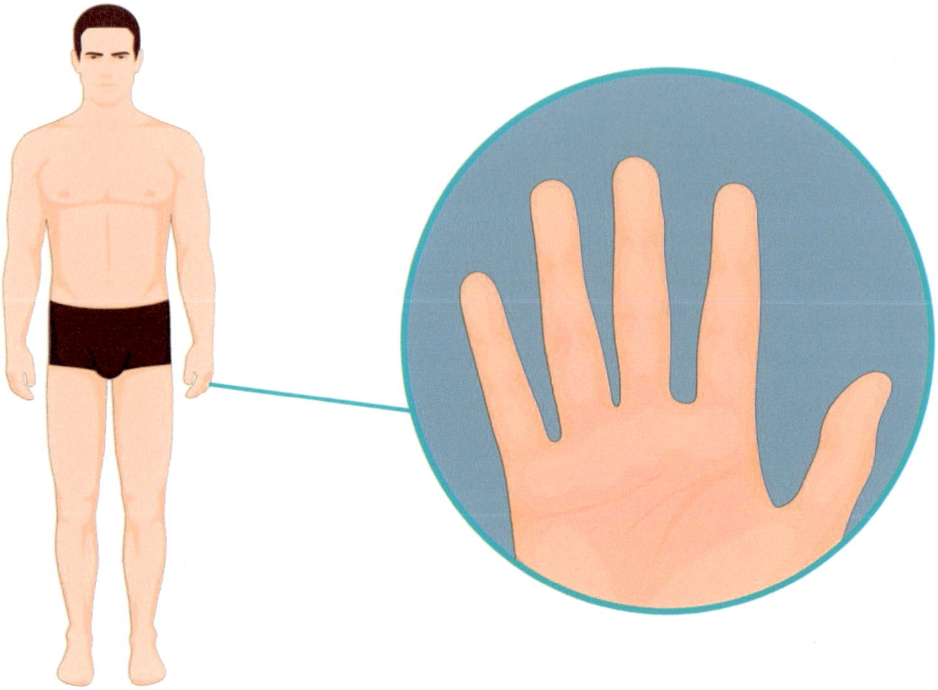

ඇඟිල්ල

ae-ngi-lla

Foot

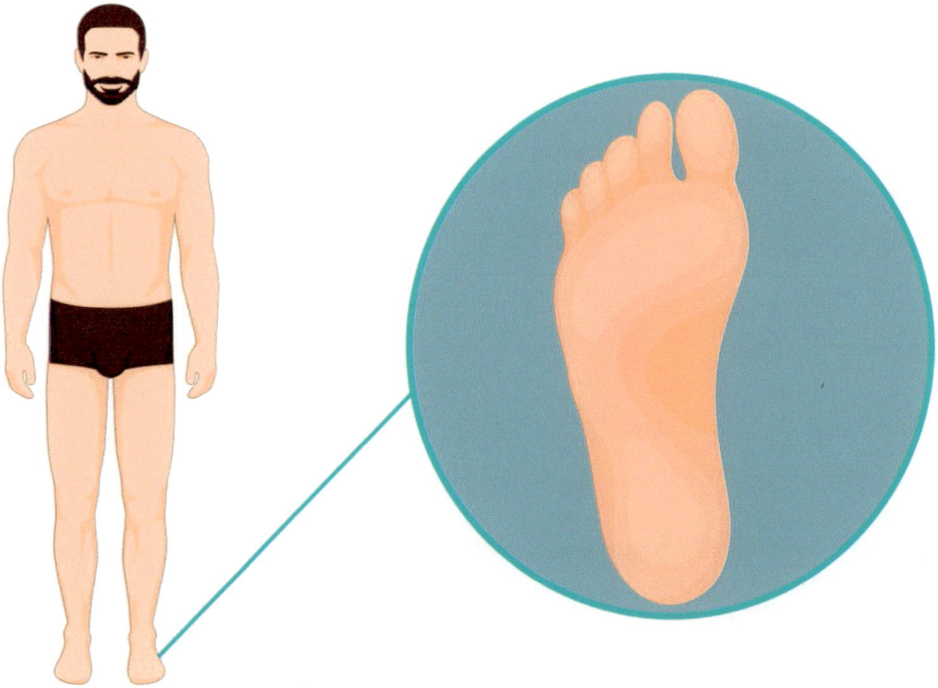

පාදය

paa-da-ya

Forehead

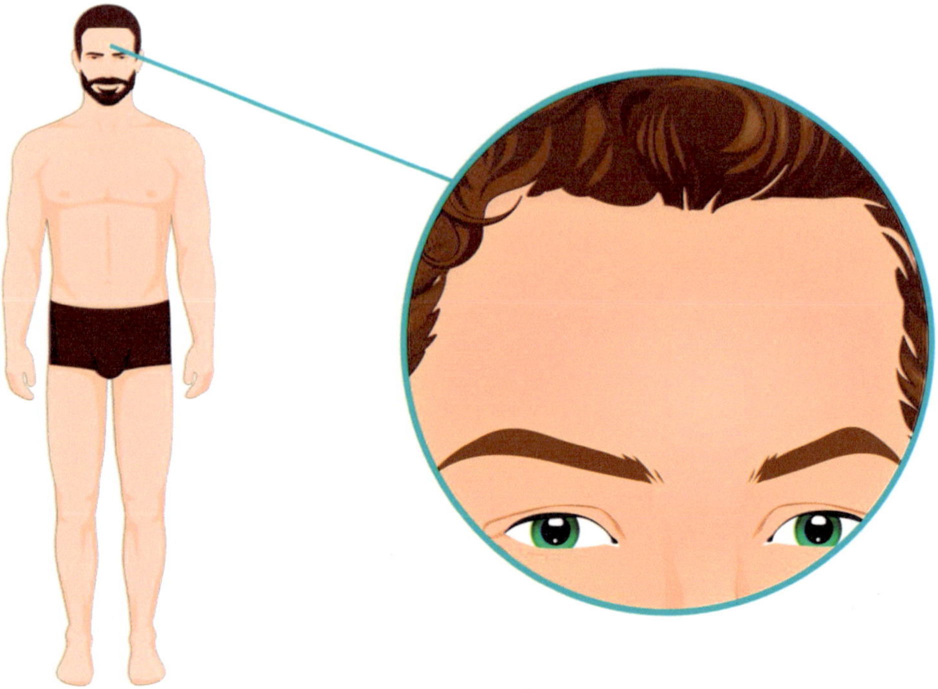

නළල

na-la-la

Hair

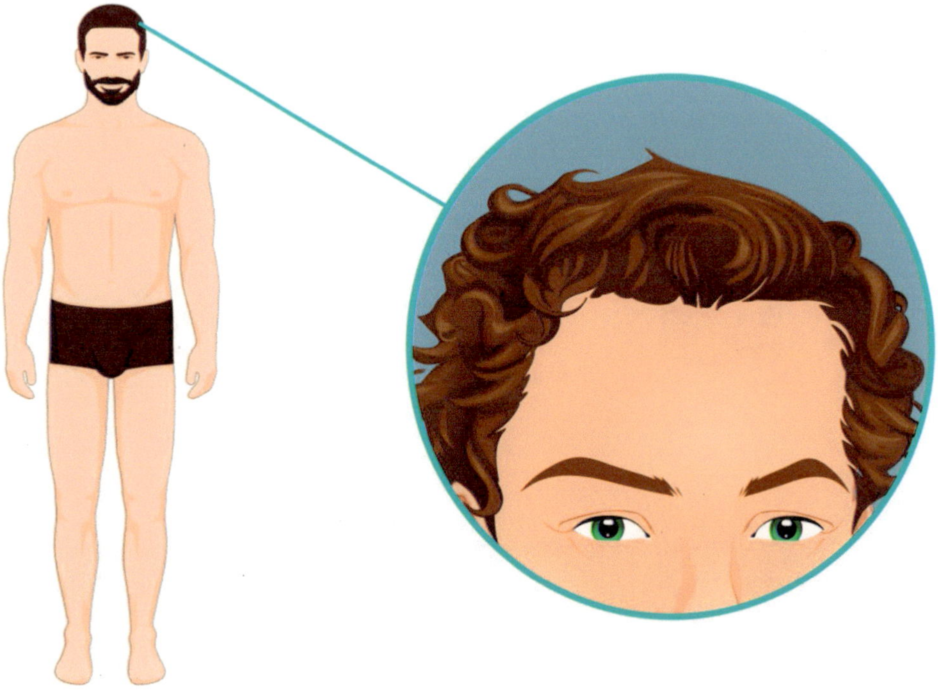

කොණ්ඩය

kon-da-ya

Hand

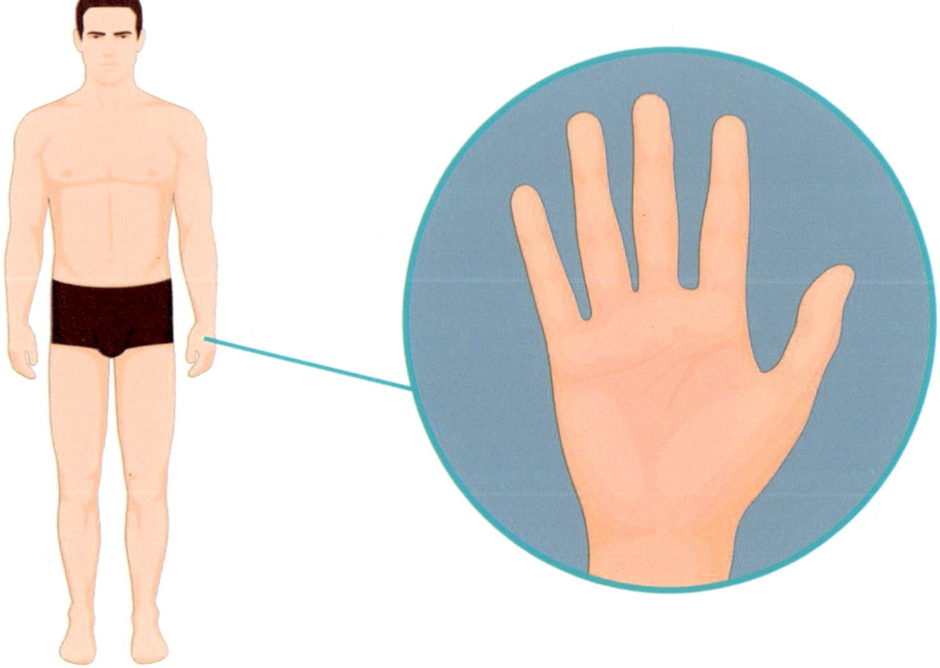

අත

atha

Head

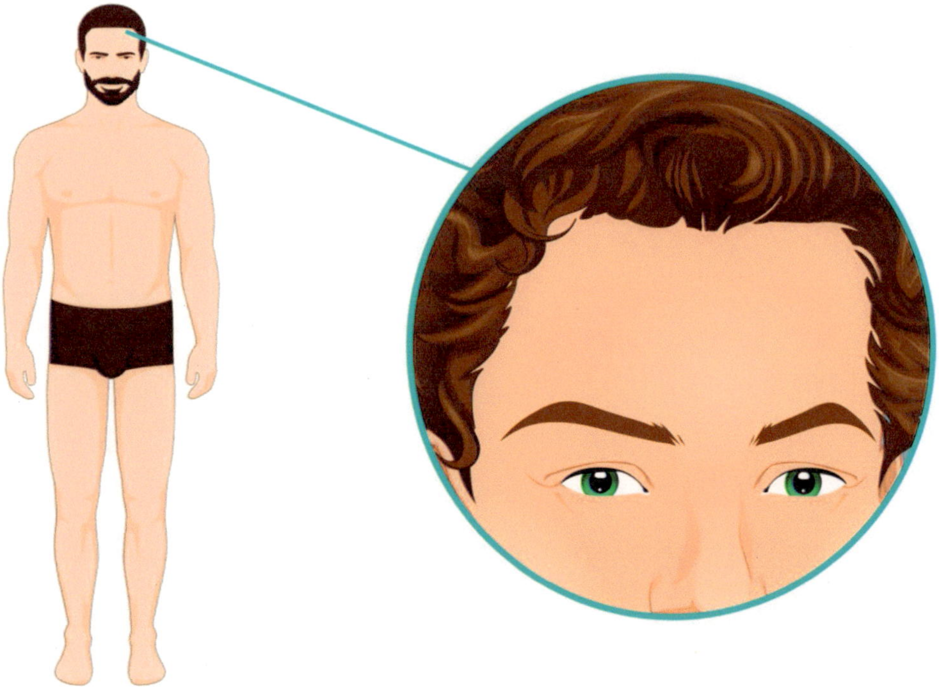

හිස

hi-sa

Heart

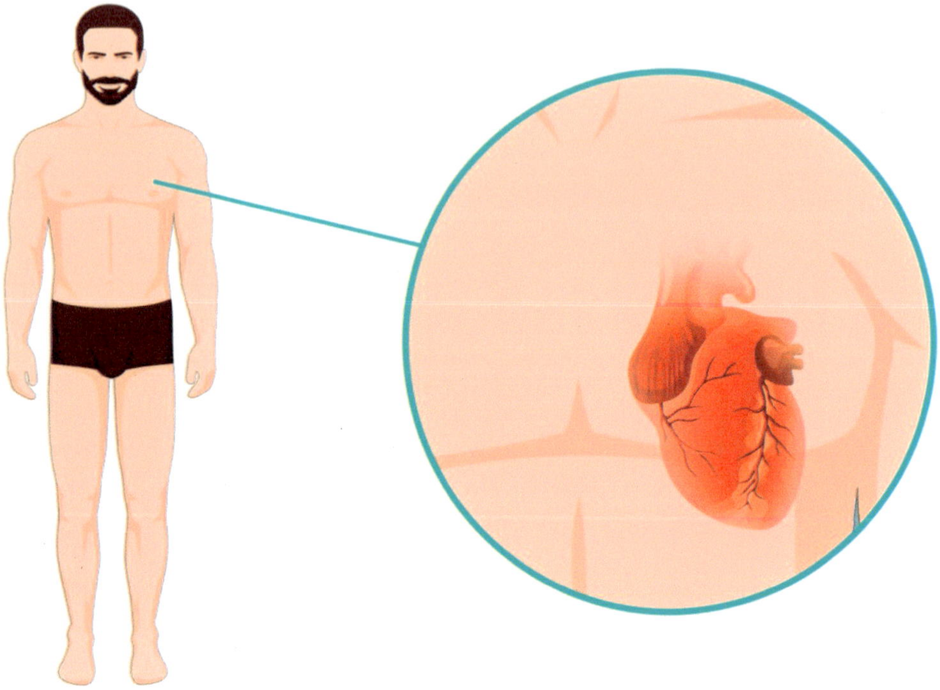

හදවත

ha-da-wa-tha

Heel

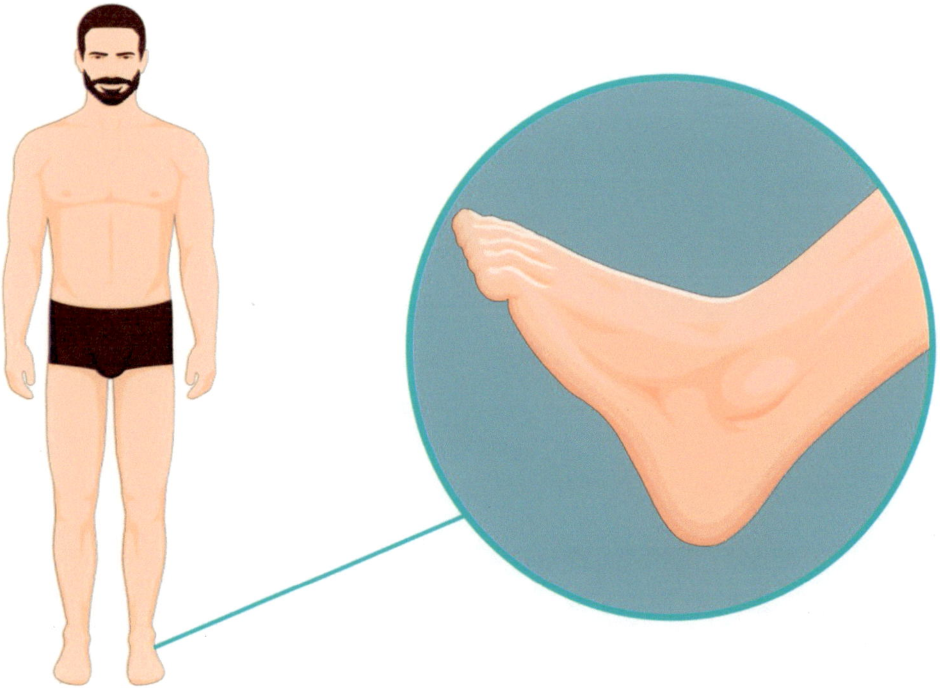

විලුඹ

vi-lum-ba

Knee

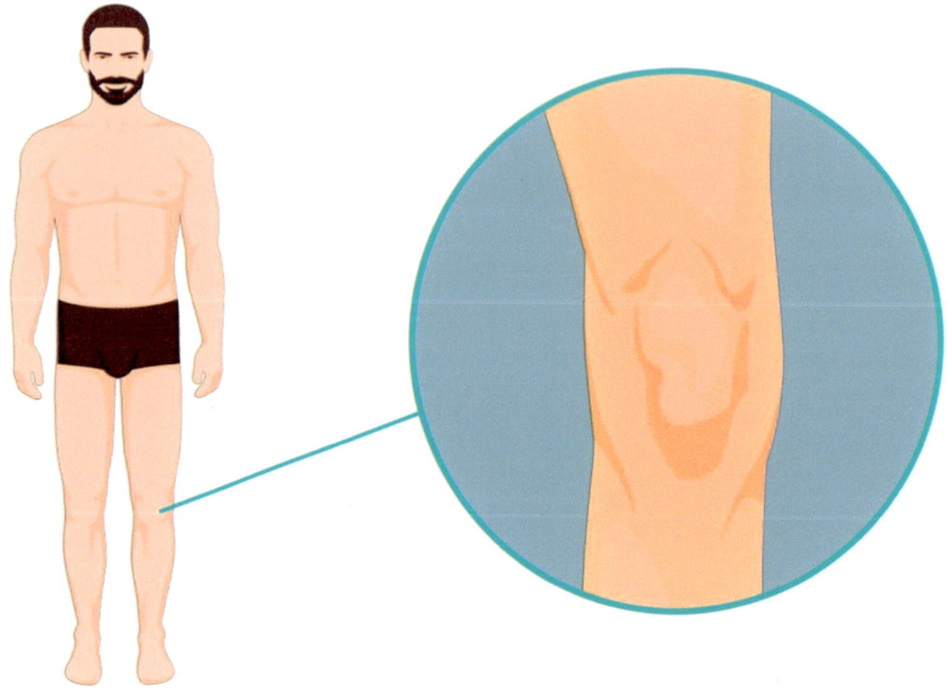

දණහිස

da-na-hi-sa

Leg

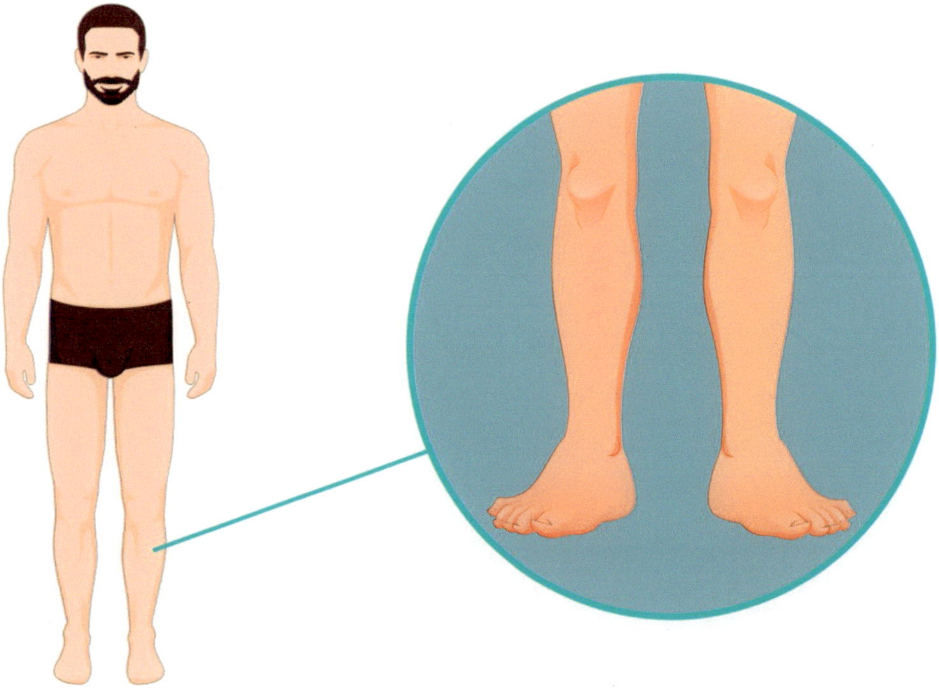

කකුල

ka-ku-la

Lip

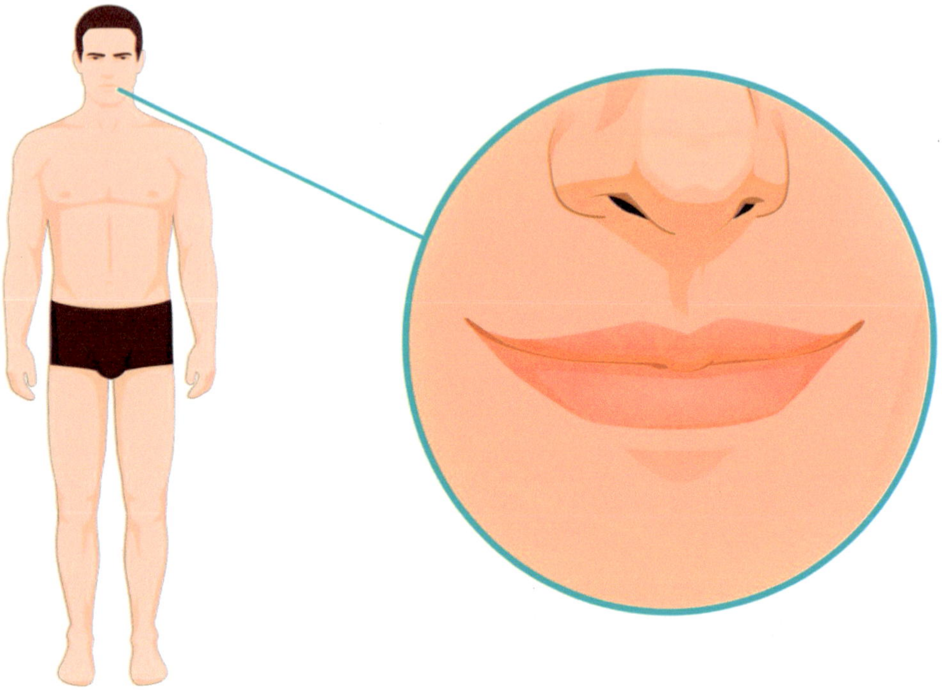

තොල

tho-la

Moustache

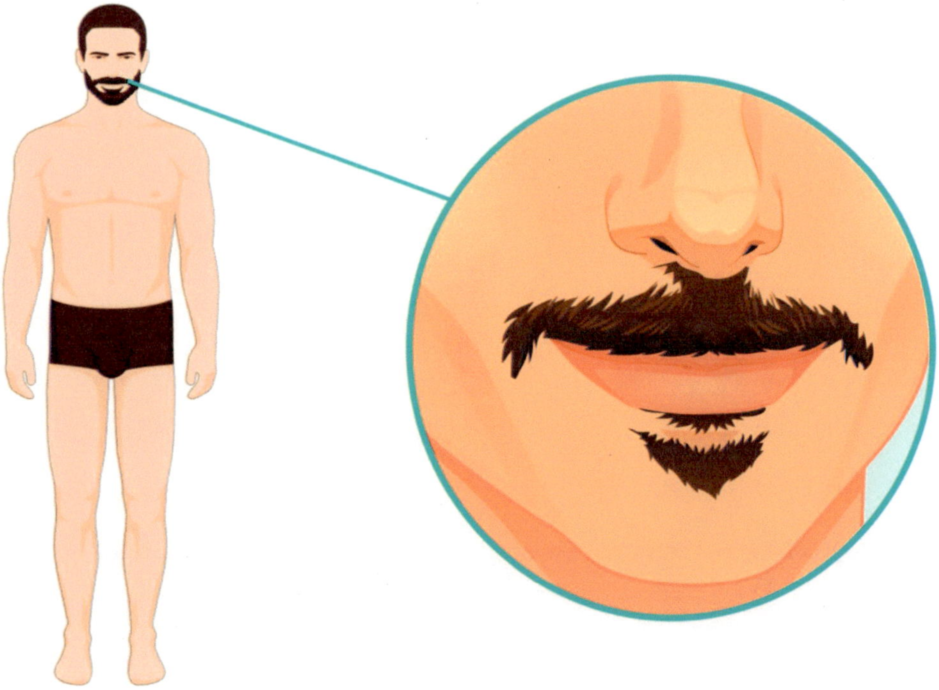

උඩුරැවුල

u-du-ra-vu-la

Mouth

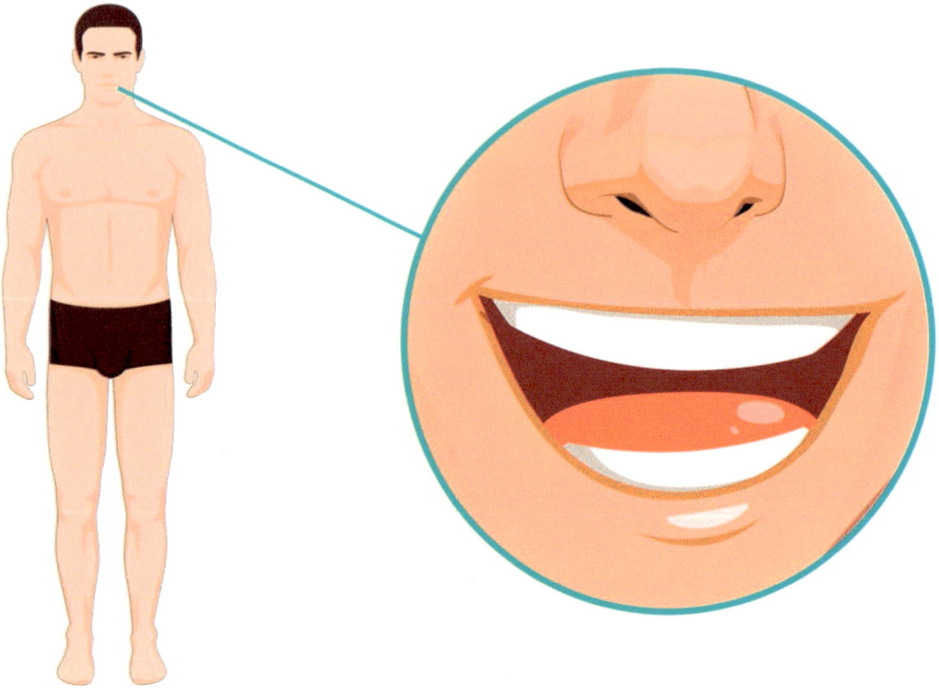

කට

ka-ta

Nail

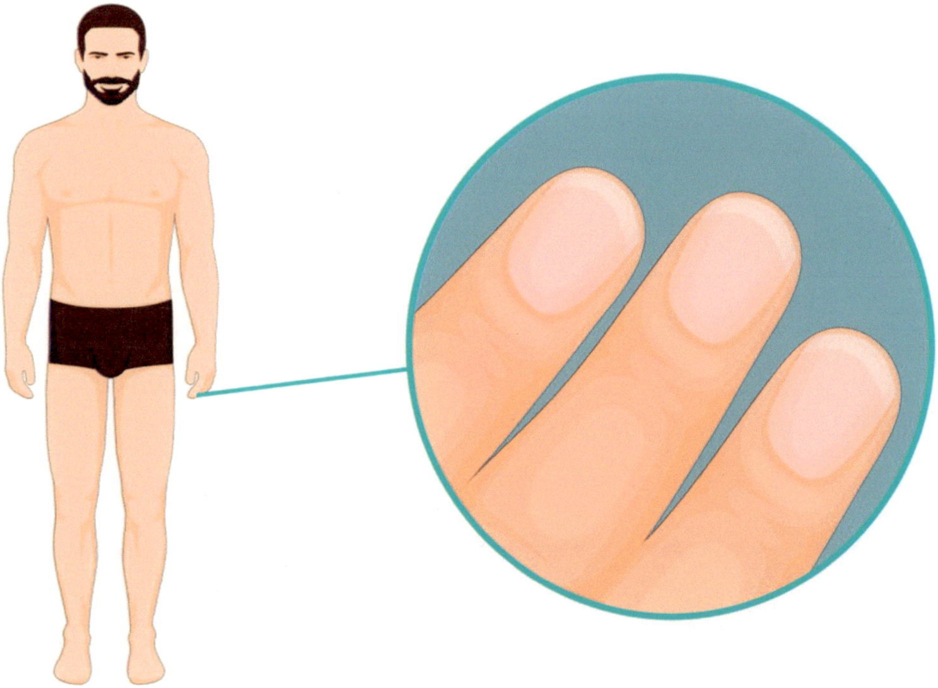

නියපොත්ත

ni-ya-poth-tha

Neck

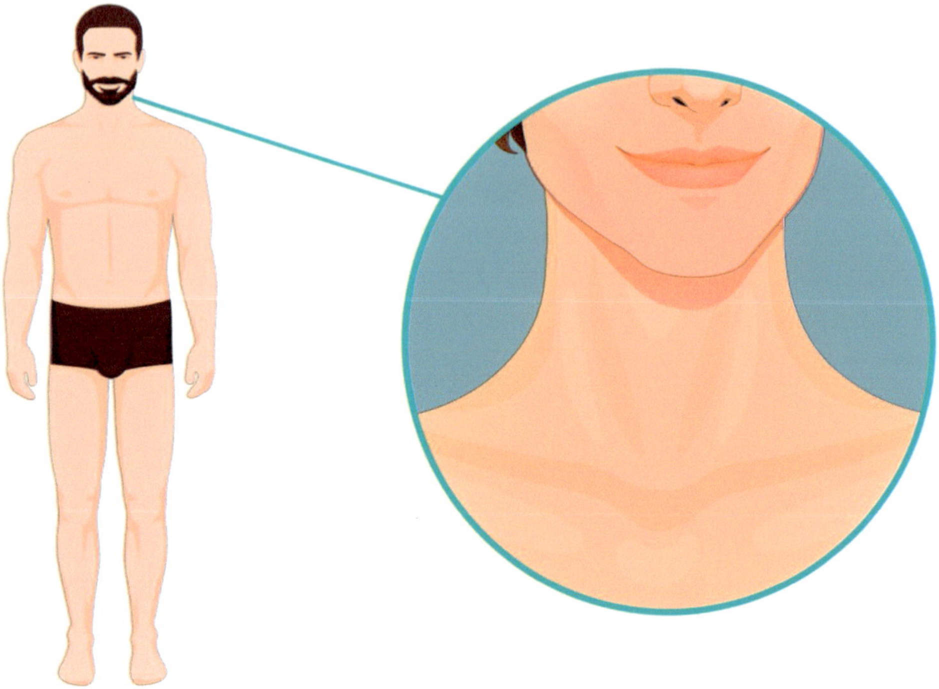

බෙල්ල

bel-la

Nose

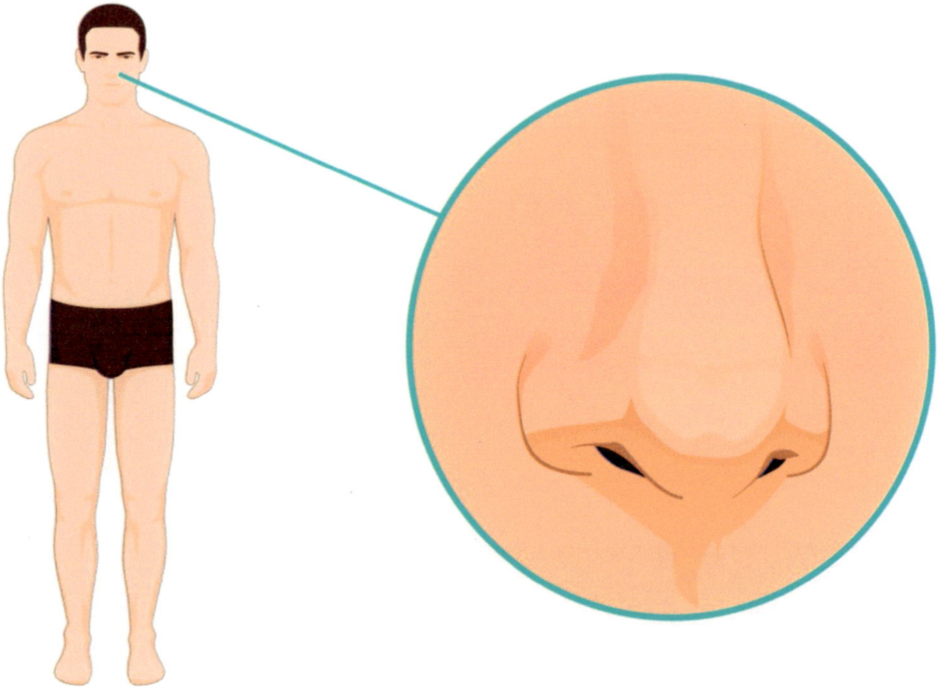

නාසය

naa-sa-ya

Shoulder

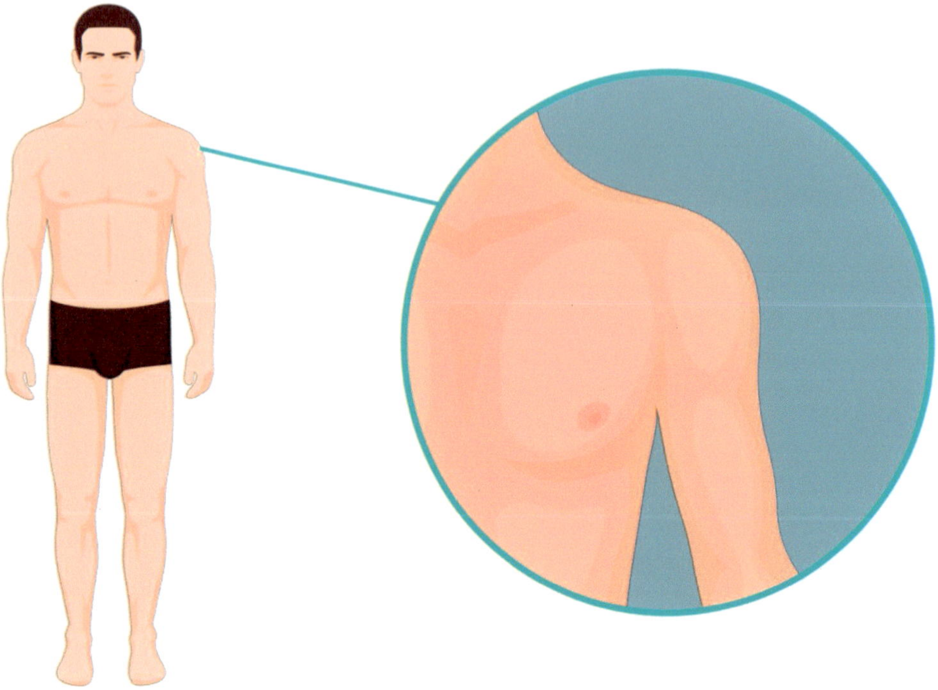

උරහිස

u-ra-hi-sa

Skin

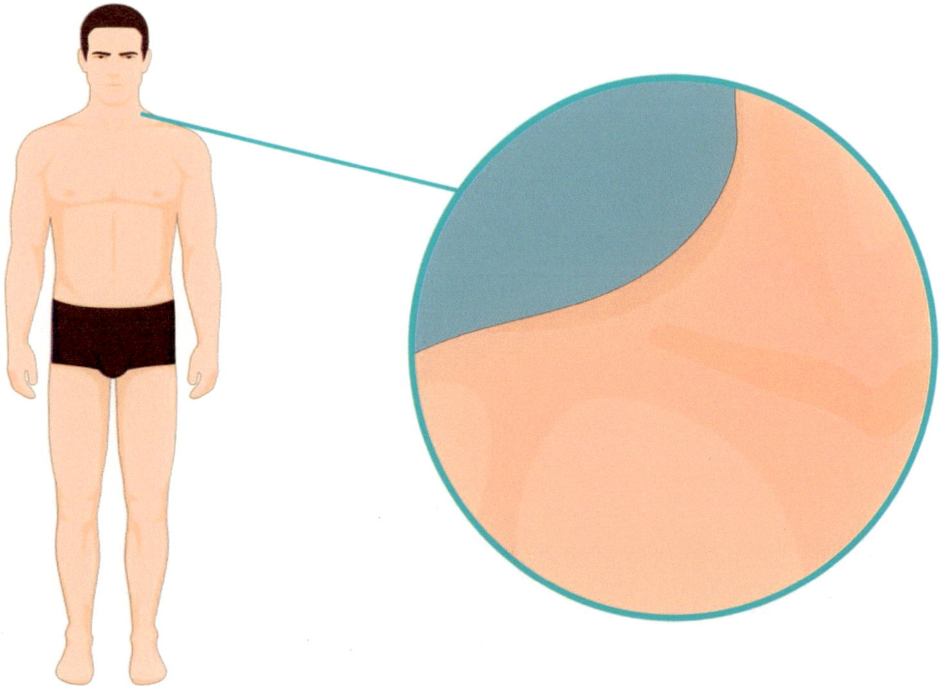

සම

sama

Stomach

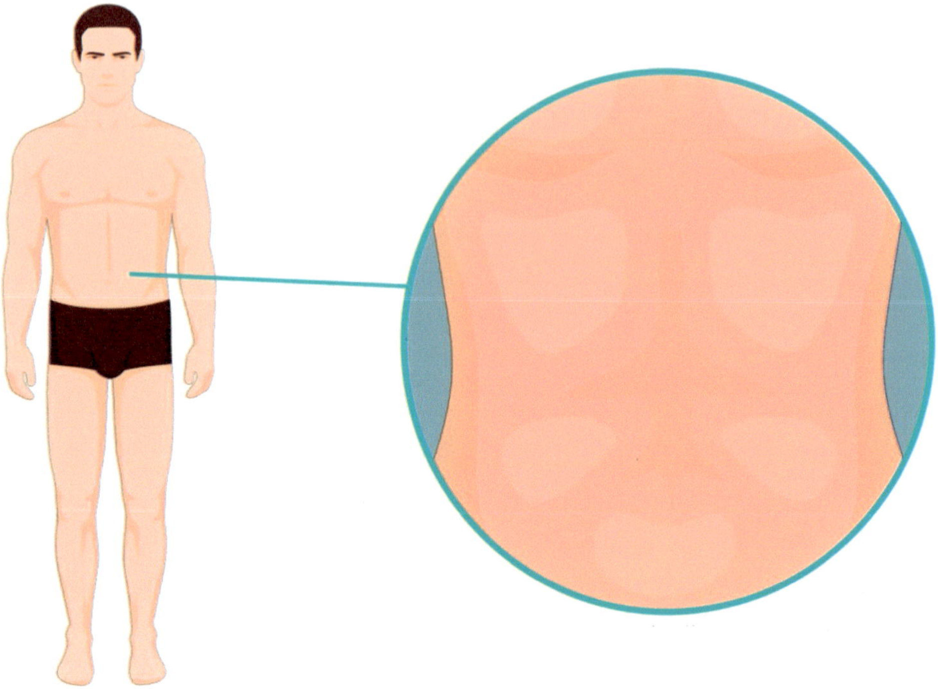

බඩ

ba-da

Thumb

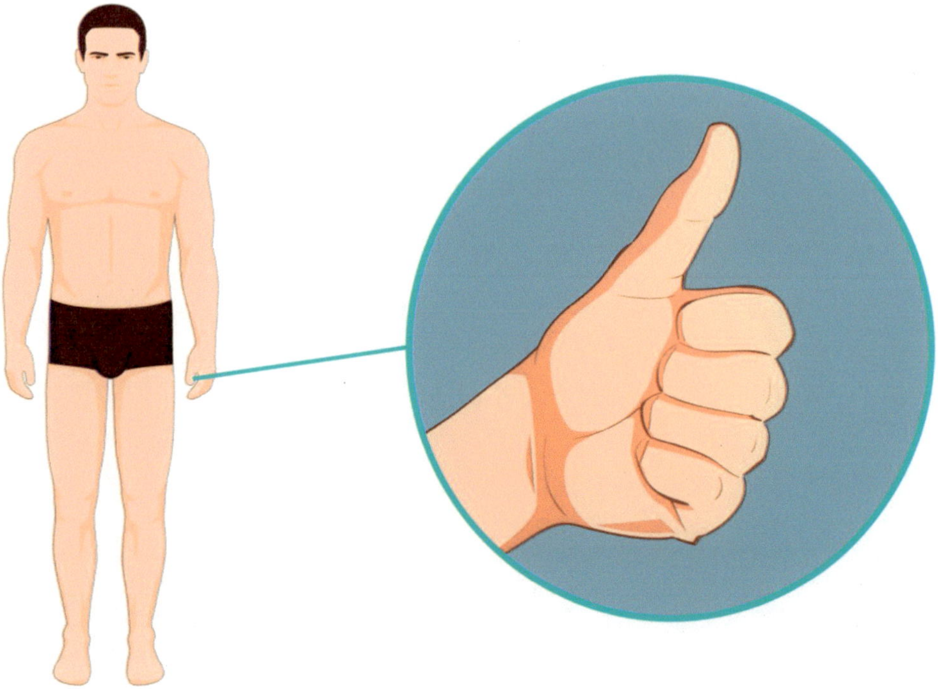

මාපටැඟිල්ල

maa-pa-tae-ngi-lla

Tongue

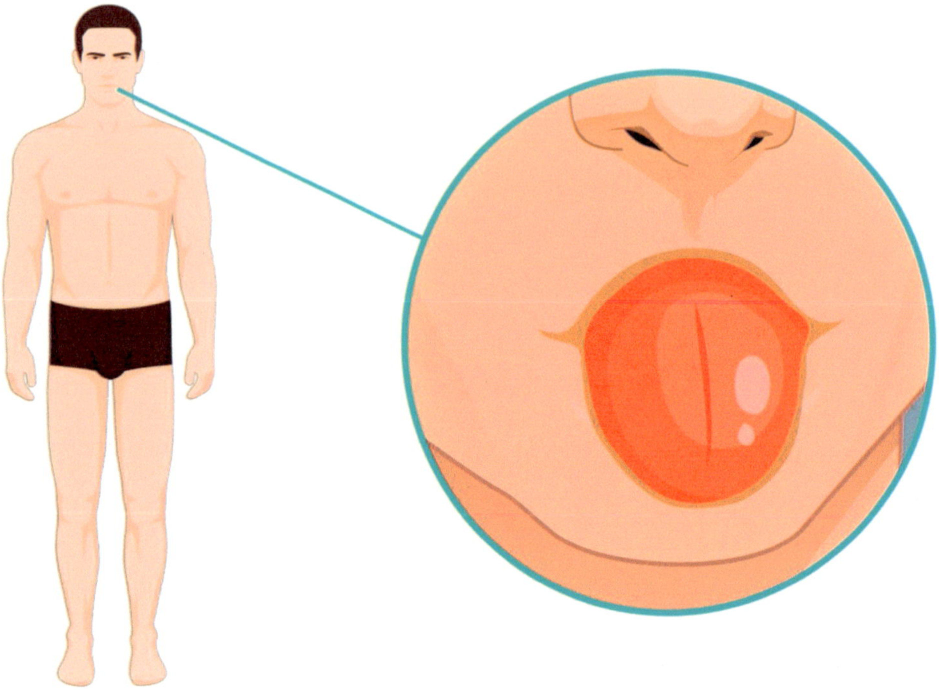

දිව

di-va

Tooth

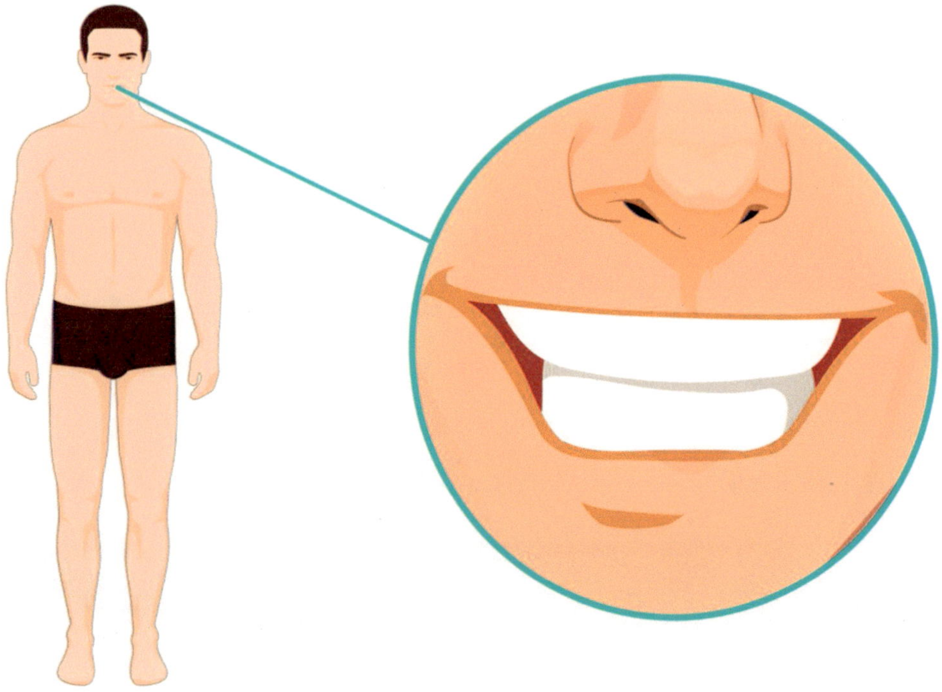

දත

da-tha

Wrist

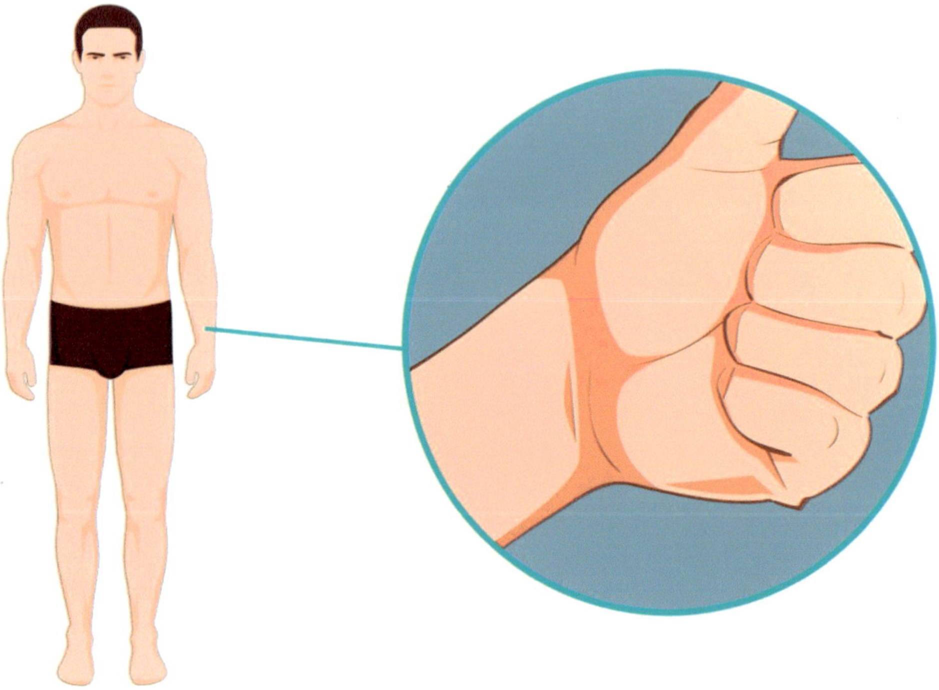

මැණික් කටුව

mae-nik-ka-tu-wa